Fat Bombs

60 Best, Delicious Fat Bomb Recipes
You Absolutely Have to Try!

© Copyright 2017 by Mark Evans - All rights reserved.

The following Book is reproduced below with the goal of providing information that is as accurate and as reliable as possible. Regardless, purchasing this Book can be seen as consent to the fact that both the publisher and the author of this book are in no way experts on the topics discussed within, and that any recommendations or suggestions made herein are for entertainment purposes only. Professionals should be consulted as needed before undertaking any of the action endorsed herein.

This declaration is deemed fair and valid by both the American Bar Association and the Committee of Publishers Association and is legally binding throughout the United States.

Furthermore, the transmission, duplication or reproduction of any of the following work, including precise information, will be considered an illegal act, irrespective whether it is done electronically or in print. The legality extends to creating a secondary or tertiary copy of the work or a recorded copy and is only allowed with express written consent of the Publisher. All additional rights are reserved.

The information in the following pages is broadly considered to be a truthful and accurate account of facts, and as such any inattention, use or misuse of the information in question by the reader will render any resulting actions solely under their purview. There are no scenarios in which the publisher or the original author of this work can be in any fashion deemed liable for any hardship or damages that may befall them after undertaking information described herein.

Additionally, the information found on the following pages is intended for informational purposes only and should thus be considered, universal. As befitting its nature, the information presented is without assurance regarding its continued validity or interim quality. Trademarks that mentioned are done without written consent and can in no way be considered an endorsement from the trademark holder.

Contents

INTRODUCTION 1

FREE BONUS BOOK 4

CHAPTER 1 – THE ESSENCE OF A LOW-CARB DIET AND FAT BOMBS 6

CHAPTER 2 – EASY-TO-DO HEALTHY FAT BOMB RECIPES 19

    Cocoa Almond Delight Fat Bombs 21

    Toffee and Peanut Butter Fat Bombs 23

    Creamy Almond Fat Bombs 25

    Chocolatey Coconut Fat Bombs 27

    Very Mocha Fat Bombs 29

    Creamy White Bombs 31

    Dark Choco Truffles 33

    Lemon Squares Keto Bombs 35

    Vanilla and Nutmeg Keto Treats 36

    Spiced Pumpkin Fat Bombs 38

    Choco Coconut Flakes Fat Bombs 40

    Peanut Butter Keto Bombs 42

    Spiced Cheesy Keto Treats 44

Coco-Vanilla Bombs 46

Baked Cheesy Jell-O Flat Bomb Cookies 47

Minty Layered Fat Bombs 49

Cheesy Bacon Bombs 51

No-Bake Red Cheesecake Bombs 53

Mediterranean-Inspired Fat Bombs 55

Lemon Keto Bombs 57

Double Chocolate Keto Bombs 58

Guacamole Healthy Treats 60

Pecan and Bacon Keto Treats 62

Coco-Choco Candy Cups 63

Egg-Free Mini Lemony Tarts 65

Choco Candies with Coconut 68

Yummy Keto Rolo 70

Frozen Cocoa Bombs 73

Fudgy White Choco Bombs 75

Spiced Keto Candies 77

Low-Carb Chocolate Bars 79

Double Chocolate Truffles 81

Cheesy Almond Keto Bombs 84

CHAPTER 3 – LOW-CARB FAT BOMB RECIPES WITH BERRIES 87

Coconut and Berries Fat Bombs 93

Chocolatey Strawberry Swirl Bombs 95

Blackberries and Cheese Fat Bombs 97

Blueberry and Cheese Fat Bombs 99

Raspberry and Choco Treats 101

Low-Carb Strawberry Cheesecake Delights 104

CHAPTER 4 – LOW-CARB FAT BOMB RECIPES WITH NUTS 107

Chewy Bombs with Macadamia 112

Walnut Keto Delights 114

Orange and Nuts Low-Carb Delights 116

Choco-Macadamia Treats 118

Pumpkin Treats with Pecans 119

Nutty Choco Treats 121

Macadamia Coconut Bombs 123

Pecan Treats with Stuffing 125

Choco Walnut Delight Bombs 127

Spiced Pistachio Fast Bombs 129

CHAPTER 5 - KETOGENIC SPECIFIC FAT BOMB RECIPES 131

Basic Fat Bomb Recipe 138

Walnut Keto Treats 140

Lemon-Flavored Cheesecake Bombs 142

Breakfast Truffles 143

Energy-Boosting Bulletproof Bombs 145

Coco Butter Bombs with Nutmeg......................... 147

Nutty Vanilla Truffles 149

Spicy Keto Bombs.. 151

Vanilla-Macadamia Healthy Bombs..................... 152

Cheesy Raspberry Keto Bombs 154

Healthy Macha Bombs 156

Chewy Keto Treats 159

CONCLUSION..161

THANK YOU! 163

Introduction

I want to thank you and congratulate you for purchasing the book, *"Fat Bombs: Sub- 60 Best, Delicious Fat Bomb Recipes You Absolutely Have to Try!"*

This is not your ordinary recipe book. Aside from the 60 healthy and delicious fat bomb recipes, it explains the basics about the low-carb diet. It aims to educate you on what you need to know about the diet while you learn how to prepare a variety of fat bomb recipes. These fat bombs are an essential part of any low-carb diet. They help you in reaching your daily required macros without going overboard.

This book explains the following aspects of a low-carb diet:

- The importance of fat bombs in the diet. It explains the most common ingredients

used in making fat bombs and their health benefits.
- The right foods to eat when following this kind of diet. Each chapter gives you an idea of the ingredients to use in preparing your meals, including the fat bombs.
- What is the state of ketosis and what can you do to stay at it for a longer period. It also has a dedicated chapter of fat bomb recipes that you can eat to maintain this state.
- The health benefits and common side effects of a low-carb diet.

The fat bomb recipes contain nutrition information that you can use as a guide. It also offers the following details:

- The idea behind these treats.
- The basic ingredients needed to make them.
- The fats and sweeteners that you can use in making fat bombs.

Thanks again for purchasing this book, I hope you enjoy it!

FREE BONUS BOOK

As a Thank You for purchasing this book, I would like to offer you another book as a special bonus! It is called "Super Foods For Super Health".

This comprehensive book is for those who are interested in:

- Learning more about super foods that you can easily get your hands on today.

- How to incorporate those super foods into your everyday meals.
- Nutritional benefits for each super foods
- How to improve your overall health
- How to lose weight naturally
- How to reduce disease risk
- How to reverse signs of aging
- Think more clearly
- Improving your focus
- And much more..

So if you are interested in learning more about any of the above, just go to http://bit.ly/superfoods-gift and grab your free bonus book!

Chapter 1 – The Essence of a Low-Carb Diet and Fat Bombs

It is easy to make fat bombs. After you have tried certain recipes, you can make your own combinations and come up with even more variety of these healthy treats.

What is a fat bomb? It is a small treat, usually in size of a small ball, but can also be served in squares or in other shapes, depending on the molds that you use. The treat is low in carbs and high in concentrated and healthy fat. The recipes typically contain more than 85 percent of fat. Flavoring and specific fats are used in the process, such as butter, mascarpone cheese, Neufchatel cheese, cream cheese, coconut oil, and coconut butter.

You can eat this whenever your body needs to get recharged, as a snack, breakfast, or after doing a tedious activity. Fat bombs are suited for any low-carb diet, such as ketogenic and paleo. They have the healthy fat that your body needs to stay in ketosis. The best thing about these treats is that they taste good and won't make you feel that you are being deprived.

Here are some of the important things that you need to remember about fat bombs:

1. They contain a huge percentage of healthy fats, most of which solidifies fast when chilled or refrigerated. This is the reason the treats are not messy to prepare and consume despite the fats that they contain.

2. They are served in small sizes. This makes it easier to pop them into your mouth whenever you need a healthy fix. This also allows you to control the nutrients, specifically the carb content of each piece.

3. Due to the fat content, these fat bombs will melt when kept at a room temperature for a long time. To keep them for up to 2 weeks, store leftovers in

an airtight container and keep it in the fridge or freezer. If chilled, thaw them first at a room temperature for several minutes before serving.

4. You can tweak the taste of the fat bombs depending on your preference and the availability of ingredients. You can use zero-carb and low-calorie sweeteners to make sweet treats. You can add spices and herbs. You can also make savory bombs by incorporating ingredients, such as avocado and bacon, in the recipes.

5. If you are using nuts, make sure that you choose the types that don't contain too much carbs. If you are on a ketogenic diet, take note that you cannot use peanut butter. You can replace this with suitable nut butter, such as almond butter.

The basic fat bombs contain these three ingredients:

- Fat base. These are the healthy fats used as ingredients. They include coconut oil, coconut butter, cacao butter, coconut milk, and almond butter. You can also use coconut cream, which is the solid part of a can of coconut milk when refrigerated. It is safe to use butter if you can tolerate dairy. The other fats used are avocado oil, bacon fat, and ghee. For the latter, it is best to choose cultured ghee that is free of casein and lactose.

- Sweetener or flavoring. You can use various flavored syrups, cacao powder, spices, peppermint extract, sugar-free vanilla extract, salt, and dark chocolate.
- Mix-in ingredients. They give texture to the fat bombs. Some samples include shredded coconut, cacao nibs, nuts, low-carb fruit, seeds, and sugar-free crumbled bacon.

Coconut Oil

Among the fats used in making these treats, the healthiest choice is coconut oil. This is the healthiest ingredient used in making fat bombs. It makes the fat burning process faster. That fats that this oil contains do not get stored in your system. Instead, your body immediately utilizes the fats for energy. Aside from being healthy, it also gives a buttery and rich flavor to your food.

This can be used in many baking and cooking recipes. Shelf life is up to 2 years. For a healthier option, you can look for the organic type that is non-GMO and gluten-free.

Coconut oil is an essential part of any low-carb diet. It helps you lose weight by boosting your energy expenditure and reducing your hunger cravings. It is also effective in reducing the fat in the abdominal area or the visceral fat that is known as the dangerous (unhealthy) fat.

This ingredient alone has the following effects on your system:

- It lowers the risk of a heart disease by improving your cholesterol levels.

- It reduces inflammation and improves the health of your thyroid.
- It also has positive effects on your hair and skin.
- Coconut oil helps you get into the state of ketosis.

How does coconut oil help you get into ketosis? It has MCTs or medium-chain triglycerides that work by boosting your ketones. Coconut oil can supply your body with an immediate form of energy when taken orally. This is something usually done by keto-dieters who eliminate all forms of carbs from their diet.

Your body converts the MCTs in the liver into ketones. They replace glycogen as the source of your body's fuel. MCT oil is also used as a supplement that aids in ketosis.

Sweeteners

Not all sweeteners are created equal, especially when you are on a low-carb diet and you are intent on losing weight. You must teach yourself how to lessen your cravings for sweets. Use sugar alternatives occasionally. You can skip adding them to your regular meals and use them solely for treats, such as your healthy fat bomb recipes.

If you are on a very low-carb diet, stick to sweeteners with zero-carb content. As for the rest, make sure that the sweeteners are healthy and qualify for your net carb limit.

1. Stevia. The extract from this herb is used as a sugar substitute or sweetener. It is grouped in the non-nutritive sweeteners on the USDA database. It is devoid of any nutrients, vitamins and it doesn't have calories. Most of the stevia products are triple times sweeter than sugar when used in moderation. These products vary in taste. There are some that said to leave a bitter aftertaste. You should try different stevia products to test which suits your taste.

2. Inulin-based sweeteners. The most popular among this type is the chicory root inulin, which

is commercially sold as Just Like Sugar that contains orange peel, calcium, and vitamin C. The other natural sources of inulin include yacon, jicama, onion, banana, Jerusalem artichoke.

If you are using any of these ingredients, be sure to avoid adding other sweeteners. Inulin is beneficial not only to people on a low-carb diet but also for diabetics because of its beneficial effect on blood sugar. Unlike stevia, inulin has certain side effects because it feeds both the good and bad bacteria. This can cause digestive issues when you consume more than the daily dose of 20 grams.

3. Erythritol. This is a sugar alcohol naturally found in fermented foods, vegetables, and fruits. It has no calories and does not have any effects on your blood glucose. Take a daily dose of 1 gram of Erythritol per kilogram of your weight to avoid side effects, such as stomach ache.

4. Xylitol. This sugar alcohol has a similar taste to sugar but contains a lower number of calories. It naturally occurs in the fibers of some veggies and

fruits. It contains low nutrients and must be used as a sweetener in moderation. Keep this out of reach of dogs because it can be toxic for your pets.

5. Dark chocolate. For your fat bombs, use the type that is made of 75 percent cacao or more with no unnecessary additives. This is a versatile ingredient. You can add this on your yogurt, baked treats, cereals, and more.

The Benefits

Fat bombs give you an instant energy boost and help you in reaching your daily nutritional requirement without going overboard. They are easy to make. You can bring them anywhere with you and pop a piece whenever hunger strikes.

They are an essential part of any low-carb diet, which requires you to eat real food and offers the following benefits:

1. Weight loss

The diet causes a decrease in your insulin levels. As a result, your kidneys will work in getting rid of the excess sodium in your system, which will lead to rapid weight loss for the first two weeks of the diet. If you do it right, you will continue to lose weight for the next 6 months. After this period, you will need to focus your attention on maintaining the weight that you have already lost. You can allow yourself to indulge on the foods that you have missed more often but always keep your carb intake in moderation.

2. Increases your good cholesterol levels

It boosts the levels of your HDL or good cholesterol and decreases the levels of your LDL or bad cholesterol. This is due to the limited amount of sugar and high amount of saturated fat that your system is getting. To ensure the health of your heart, you need to maintain above 39 mg HDL over your LDL. This will prevent arterial blockage and reduce your risk of inflammation.

3. Suppressed appetite

The ketone bodies and your intake of fat will make you feel full most of the time. They will take your mind away from eating. A low-carb diet effectively reduces your food cravings. It is important that you eat even though you are not hungry. Your body needs to work on something to give your body sufficient energy. You still need to eat to meet your daily required macros.

4. Lower blood pressure

This is effective in keeping your blood pressure at a normal rate but a low-carb diet is not advisable for those who are already taking medications for this condition. Talk to your doctor first if you want to proceed with the diet. People who are taking medications for high blood pressure often experience dizziness as a side effect of the diet.

5. Instant energy boost

The diet improves your sleeping patterns, which will make you feel energized at the start of the day. At times when you are feeling drained, you simply need to eat or pop a piece or two of fat bombs and you will instantly have an energy boost. The diet can also help in improving chronic fatigue. It prohibits eating grains and grain-based foods, which result to the relief of joint and muscle pain and stiffness.

6. Clearer mind

The first few days of the diet are the hardest. Your body is still getting used to the scheme of things – how you eat and what you are eating. After you have gotten used to it, your body will get keto-adapted. This will result to a better way of thinking.

7. Other health benefits

The diet is said to improve gut health and digestion. It also prevents epileptic seizures. It improves the health of your brain and gives you a better mood most of the time. There are certain studies, which proved that a low-carb diet can help in improving brain-related cases, such as ALS, Alzheimer's, and Parkinson's.

Chapter 2 – Easy-to-Do Healthy Fat Bomb Recipes

Fat bombs are easy to make as long as you have the complete ingredients and you are equipped with the right tools. Some recipes will require the use of a food processor or blender. An electric hand mixer will also come in handy. Most fat bombs are refrigerated or frozen, and there are only a few that needs to be baked in an oven.

You can opt to use your hands to form your dough into small balls. You can also use baking pans or trays lined with wax or parchment paper, or lightly greased, as molds. After the fat bomb has firmed, you can cut them into squares or rectangular pieces. You can also get creative and use molds intended for candies or cupcakes. You can also turn your fat bombs into cake pops by placing them on sticks and dipping them in melted dark chocolate before adding texture and decorations.

Fat bombs are usually made by following these three steps:

1. Put all the ingredients in a bowl, blender, or a food processor. Process until you have attained the required consistency. If you are using solid fat, melt it on low heat or microwave for a few seconds.

2. Transfer the mixture into molds or put them in any container and cover with plastic before you freeze or refrigerate the mixture for several hours or overnight.

3. Slice the fat bombs or use your hands to shape them into small balls.

Now put what you have learned into practice. Begin with the following easy-to-make recipes that you can snack on any time of the day.

Cocoa Almond Delight Fat Bombs

Servings: 24 pieces

Nutrition facts per piece: Calories 145 kcal, Fats 14.7 g, Protein 1.53 g, Net carb 1.1 g

Ingredients:

- 3 tablespoons cocoa
- 9 1/2 tablespoons almond butter
- 3/8 teaspoon (60 drops) liquid stevia
- 3/4 cup melted coconut oil
- 9 tablespoons melted salted butter

Directions:

1. Mix all the ingredients in a bowl until combined.

2. Prepare lightly greased mini muffin molds with 24 holes. Pour 2 tablespoons of the mixture into each hole. Freeze for half an hour or until set.

3. Carefully pop out the fat bombs from the molds and transfer to an airtight container. Serve immediately. Put back any leftover in the fridge.

Toffee and Peanut Butter Fat Bombs

Servings: 24 pieces

Nutrition facts per piece: Calories 142 kcal, Fats 15 g, Protein 2 g, Net carb 0.9 g

Ingredients:

- 4 ounces cream cheese
- 1 cup coconut oil
- 3/4 tablespoons cocoa butter
- 2 tablespoons butter
- 3 tablespoons unsweetened toffee syrup
- 1/2 cup natural peanut butter

Directions:

1. Put all the ingredients in a pan over medium-low heat. Stir until melted and combined.

2. Transfer the mixture into greased molds like a mini muffin pan. Freeze for 30 minutes. Pop and serve.

3. Put any leftovers in an airtight container and refrigerate until ready to serve.

Creamy Almond Fat Bombs

Servings: 8 pieces

Nutrition facts per piece: Calories 214 kcal, Fats 22 g, Protein 5 g, Net carb 2 g

Ingredients:

- 2 teaspoons cocoa powder
- 4 tablespoons coconut oil
- 10 tablespoons almond butter
- 1/4 teaspoon allspice
- 6 drops of liquid stevia (adjust according to taste)
- 5 tablespoons heavy cream

Directions:

1. Put the almond butter into the mold that you are using. Add the rest of the ingredients. Mix thoroughly until combined. Freeze for a couple of hours.

2. Remove from the mold. Slice and serve. You can sprinkle chopped almonds on top if preferred.

Chocolatey Coconut Fat Bombs

Servings: 12 squares

Nutrition facts per piece: Calories 237 kcal, Fats 31 g, Protein 4 g, Net carb 1.3 g

Ingredients:

- 2 tablespoons cocoa powder
- 2 tablespoons honey
- A pinch of sea salt
- 2 cups of unsweetened shredded coconut
- 4 ounces cream cheese
- 1 cup coconut oil
- 1/4 teaspoon cinnamon
- Sugar substitute to taste

Directions:

1. Heat coconut oil in a pan over medium flame. Stir in the rest of the ingredients except for the cocoa powder and cream cheese. Mix until combined.

2. Pour the mixture into a pan lined with wax paper. Spread out and press to make an even layer. Cover the pan and freeze for an hour.

3. Put the cream cheese and cocoa powder in a pan over low heat. Mix until melted and combined. Pour the mixture on top of the solid layer of your fat bombs. Freeze for 15 minutes.

4. Slice and serve.

Very Mocha Fat Bombs

Servings: 6 pieces

Nutrition facts per piece: Calories 167 kcal, Fats 19 g, Protein 0.1 g, Net carb 0.9 g

Ingredients:

- 12 teaspoons Splenda
- 4 tablespoons coconut oil
- 4 tablespoons grass-fed butter
- 1 tablespoon cocoa powder
- 2 tablespoons heavy cream
- 1/2 teaspoon coffee extract

Directions:

1. Put the butter in a heatproof bowl. Microwave until soft. Add the heavy cream and mix until combined. Leave to cool.

2. In another bowl, combine the coffee extract, cocoa powder, sweetener, and coconut oil.

3. Spread out the butter and cream mixture at the bottom of a greased pan. Refrigerate for 15 minutes to set. Pour the mocha mixture on top. Freeze for half an hour.

4. Remove from the pan. Slice and serve.

Creamy White Bombs

Servings: 2 slices

Nutrition facts per piece: Calories 170 kcal, Fats g, Protein g, Net carb 1.5 g

Ingredients:

- 1/8 teaspoon cinnamon
- 1/2 cup creamed coconut (sliced into squares)

For the first icing

- 1 tablespoon almond butter
- 1 tablespoon extra-virgin coconut oil

For the second icing

- 1/2 teaspoon cinnamon
- 1 tablespoon almond butter

Directions:

1. Combine the cinnamon and coconut cream in a

bowl. Transfer to a baking pan lined with wax paper. Press to make an even layer.

2. In a bowl, mix the ingredients for the first icing. Pour this over the first layer. Freeze for 10 minutes.

3. Whisk all the ingredients for the second icing in a bowl. Drizzle this over the frozen fat bomb. Freeze for at least 5 minutes. Slice and serve.

Dark Choco Truffles

Servings: 2 dozens

Nutrition facts per 3 pieces: Calories 292 kcal, Fats 31 g, Protein 2.2 g, Net carb 1.3 g

Ingredients:

For the chocolate coating

- 1 tablespoon Swerve confectioners powder
- 2 ounces unsweetened baking chocolate
- 1/4 teaspoon sugar-free vanilla extract
- 1/2 ounce of cocoa butter
- 1/8 teaspoon of artificial sweetener

For the ganache filling

- 5 ounces of low-carb chocolate
- 1/2 teaspoon chocolate extract
- 1 1/4 teaspoons of chocolate extract
- 2 tablespoons plus 2 teaspoons of heavy cream

Directions:

1. To make the ganache, melt the chocolate in a double boiler.

2. Put the cream and vanilla in a heatproof bowl. Microwave for 2 minutes. Add the melted chocolate. Mix until combined. Leave for 5 minutes. Cover the bowl with a plastic wrap. Freeze for 5 hours or overnight.

3. Form the ganache into balls using your hands. Arrange them on a tray lined with wax paper. Refrigerate to set.

4. Mix the chocolate and butter in a double boiler over low heat. Add the sweeteners and vanilla. Dip each ball into the melted coating. You can hold the ball with a fork or toothpick. Allow the coating to set before serving.

Lemon Squares Keto Bombs

Servings: 16 squares

Nutrition facts per piece: Calories 112 kcal, Fats 11.9 g, Protein 0.76 g, Net carb 0.8 g

Ingredients:

- 7.1 ounces of coconut butter (softened)
- 1/4 cup extra virgin coconut oil (softened)
- A pinch of salt
- 2 teaspoons of lemon extract
- 20 drops of sweetener

Directions:

1. Mix all the ingredients in a bowl until combined. Pour into a pan lined with parchment paper. Refrigerate for 2 hours. Slice and serve.

Note: Instead of lemon, you can tweak the flavor of this recipe by using other extracts, such as herbs, fruits, and vanilla.

Vanilla and Nutmeg Keto Treats

Servings: 12 pieces

Nutrition facts per piece: Calories 57 kcal, Fats 5.3 g, Protein 0.55 g, Net carb 0.8 g

Ingredients:

- 1 cup shredded coconut
- 1 cup full-fat coconut milk
- 1 teaspoon artificial sweetener
- 1/2 teaspoon cinnamon
- 1/2 teaspoon nutmeg
- 1 teaspoon vanilla extract
- 1 cup coconut butter

Directions:

1. Put all the ingredients except for the shredded coconut in a bowl. Put the bowl in a double boiler over low heat. Gradually mix the ingredients until combined and melted. Remove from heat and

leave to cool. Cover the bowl and freeze for 2 hours.

2. Form balls from the mixture. Roll them in the shredded coconut. Arrange in a tray and put in the fridge for an hour or two.

3. Serve and enjoy.

Spiced Pumpkin Fat Bombs

Servings: 6 pieces

Nutrition facts per piece: Calories 216 kcal, Fats 24 g, Protein 0.1 g, Net carb 1 g

Ingredients:

- ½ cup pumpkin
- 4 tablespoons coconut oil
- 8 tablespoons unsalted butter
- Liquid stevia to taste
- Ginger, cinnamon, nutmeg, and clove to taste

Directions:

1. Put the coconut oil in a heatproof bowl. Microwave until melted and hot. Add butter and mix until combined. Continue mixing as you gradually add the pumpkin. Add the spices and stevia. Mix until smooth and creamy.

2. Transfer the mixture to a pan lined with parchment paper. Refrigerate until set. Roll into 1-inch balls and arrange on a tray. Refrigerate for an hour before serving.

Choco Coconut Flakes Fat Bombs

Servings: 6 pieces

Nutrition facts per piece: Calories 372 kcal, Fats 40 g, Protein 2 g, Net carb 6 g

Ingredients:

- 3 ounces unsweetened baking chocolate
- 5 ounces coconut oil
- ¼ teaspoon salt
- 3 ounces unsalted butter
- Liquid stevia to taste
- 1 ½ tablespoons cocoa powder
- 3 tablespoons unsweetened coconut flakes (big flakes)

Directions:

1. Preheat oven to 350 degrees. Spread out the coconut flakes on a baking sheet and toast. Check often to make sure they don't get burned or overcooked.

2. Put the unsalted butter, unsweetened dark chocolate, and coconut oil in a heatproof bowl. Microwave for 2 minutes. Stir in the salt, stevia, and cocoa. Pour into your preferred mold. Press the coconut flakes on top. Freeze until set.

3. Immediately store any leftovers in the fridge to prevent them from melting.

Peanut Butter Keto Bombs

Servings: 10 pieces

Nutrition facts per piece: Calories 184 kcal, Fats 20 g, Protein 2 g, Net carb 1 g

Ingredients:

- 1/4 cup peanut butter
- 1/4 cup cocoa powder
- Liquid stevia to taste
- 3/4 cup coconut oil

Directions:

1. Put coconut oil in a heatproof bowl. Microwave for a few seconds until melted. Divide this into 3 bowls.

2. Add peanut butter to the first bowl with coconut oil. Mix until blended. Add stevia to taste. Combine the oil with cocoa powder on the next bowl. Add stevia to taste and mix well. Add stevia to the last bowl and mix until combined.

3. Transfer the mixtures into your molds. Spread out the chocolate flavored oil at the bottom. Put in the fridge for at least 10 minutes. Top it with the peanut butter layer and refrigerate until firm. Remove from the molds and pour the clear coconut oil over the fat bombs. You can opt to sprinkle them with chopped nuts or shredded coconut. Freeze until ready to serve.

Spiced Cheesy Keto Treats

Servings: 6 pieces

Nutrition facts per piece: Calories 367 kcal, Fats 61 g, Protein 14 g, Net carb 1 g

Ingredients:

- 1 teaspoon liquid stevia
- 8 ounces Neufchatel cheese (softened)
- 1/2 teaspoon nutmeg
- 1/2 teaspoon ground cloves
- 1 tablespoon cinnamon
- 1 teaspoon ginger
- 3/4 cup coconut oil

Directions:

1. Put everything in a food processor, except the coconut oil. Process at low speed. Gradually add the oil as you continue to process the mixture.

2. Divide into 6 and roll into balls. Arrange in a tray, cover, and put in the fridge for 15 minutes.

As an option, you can drizzle melted dark chocolate on top of the balls. Refrigerate until ready to serve.

Coco-Vanilla Bombs

Servings: 6 pieces

Nutrition facts per piece: Calories 138 kcal, Fats 13 g, Protein 1 g, Net carb 2 g

Ingredients:

- 2 tablespoons coconut oil
- 1 cup unsweetened shredded coconut
- 1/8 teaspoon salt
- Liquid stevia to taste
- 1/2 teaspoon vanilla extract
- 1/4 cup water

Directions:

1. Put all the ingredients in a food processor. Process until combined. Transfer to your mold and press until firm. Refrigerate for 15 minutes. Slice and serve.

Baked Cheesy Jell-O Flat Bomb Cookies

Servings: 12 pieces

Nutrition facts per piece: Calories 147 kcal, Fats 24 g, Protein 3 g, Net carb 1 g

Ingredients:

- 1 pack sugar-free Jell-O (any flavor)
- 6 ounces cream cheese
- 1/8 teaspoon sea salt
- 1 egg
- 1/2 teaspoon vanilla extract
- 1/2 teaspoon baking powder
- 1 cup almond flour
- 4 tablespoons unsalted butter (softened)
- 1/4 teaspoon almond extract
- 8 drops liquid stevia

Directions:

1. Put the softened butter and cream cheese in a bowl. Beat to combine. Add the extracts and sweetener.

2. In another bowl, combine the Jell-O powder and salt. Add the almond flour and baking powder. Mix well. Gradually add this to the cream cheese mixture. Blend using a fork. Roll the dough into a ball. Cover with a plastic wrap and refrigerate for 1 to 12 hours.

3. Form 1-inch balls from the dough. Arrange them on a baking sheet. Flatten the top of the cookies using the bottom of a glass. Bake in a preheated oven at 325 degrees for 6 minutes.

4. Allow to cool completely before serving. Avoid touching before cookies are completely cooled because they might crumble.

Minty Layered Fat Bombs

Servings: 12 pieces

Nutrition facts per piece: Calories 155 kcal, Fats 18 g, Protein 0.1 g, Net carb 1 g

Ingredients:

- 1/3 cup coconut shreds
- 3/4 cup coconut butter
- 1/2 teaspoon peppermint extract
- Liquid stevia to taste
- 3 tablespoons coconut oil
- 2 teaspoons unsweetened cocoa powder

Directions:

1. In a bowl, put the shredded coconut, peppermint extract, a tablespoon of coconut oil, and coconut butter. Mix until combined. Pour at the bottom of your molds. Refrigerate for 15 minutes.

2. Combine the cocoa powder and coconut oil in a bowl. Pour this on top of the firm layer. Refriger-

ate until set. Leave at room temperature for 5 minutes before slicing and serving.

Cheesy Bacon Bombs

Servings: 12 pieces

Nutrition facts per piece: Calories 201 kcal, Fats 32 g, Protein 8 g, Net carb 1 g

Ingredients:

- 8 bacon slices (fried and crumbled)
- 4 teaspoons bacon fat
- 8 ounces Neufchatel cheese (softened)
- 1/4 cup sugar-free maple syrup
- 4 tablespoons coconut oil
- 1/2 cup unsalted butter

Directions:

1. Set aside a little of the crumbled bacon.

2. Put the remaining ingredients in a heatproof bowl. Microwave until melted. Stir the mixture every now and then to make sure that everything is combined. Pour into a pan and freeze for at

least 15 minutes. Sprinkle the crumbled bacon on top. Slice and serve.

No-Bake Red Cheesecake Bombs

Servings: 48 pieces

Nutrition facts per piece: Calories 81 kcal, Fats 8.6 g, Protein 1 g, Net carb 1 g

Ingredients:

- A few drops of red food color
- 3 teaspoons raspberry extract
- 8 ounces cream cheese (softened)
- 2 tablespoons heavy cream
- 1 1/2 cups sugar-free chocolate chips
- 1/2 cup of sugar substitute
- 1/4 cup coconut oil (melted)
- A pinch of salt
- 1 teaspoon vanilla stevia

Directions:

1. Combine the cream cheese and sugar substitute in a blender. Process until smooth. Add the cream, salt, stevia, food coloring, and raspberry

extract. Process until combined. Slowly add the coconut oil. Scrape the sides to make sure that the oil is distributed evenly to the mixture. Transfer to a bowl and cover with plastic. Put in the fridge for an hour or until set.

2. Use a cookie scoop to measure 1 1/4-inch size balls. Arrange in a tray. Freeze until ready to serve.

3. As an option, you can coat the balls with melted dark chocolate. Refrigerate until set.

Mediterranean-Inspired Fat Bombs

Servings: 5 pieces

Nutrition facts per piece: Calories 164 kcal, Fats 17.1 g, Protein 3.7 g, Net carb 1.7 g

Ingredients:

- 1/4 cup of softened butter
- 1/2 cup full-fat cream cheese
- 5 tablespoons grated Parmesan cheese
- 2 garlic cloves (crushed)
- 4 sun-dried tomatoes (drained)
- 4 pitted olives
- 3 tablespoons of fresh herbs (or 2 teaspoons of dried herbs)
- Freshly ground black pepper and sea salt to taste

Directions:

1. In a bowl, mash the softened butter and cream cheese using a fork until combined. Add the

herbs, tomatoes, garlic, and olives. Season with salt and pepper. Mix well. Cover the bowl and put in the fridge for at least 30 minutes.

2. Use your hands to create fat bomb balls from the dough. Roll each ball in cheese until completely covered. Arrange the balls on a tray. Refrigerate for 15 minutes before serving.

Note: For the herbs, you can use basil, oregano, or thyme.

Lemon Keto Bombs

Servings: 16 pieces

Nutrition facts per piece: Calories 112 kcal, Fats 11.9 g, Protein 0.76 g, Net carb 0.8 g

Ingredients:

- 2 tablespoons fresh lemon zest
- 7.1 ounces coconut butter (softened)
- A pinch of salt
- 15 drops of liquid stevia
- 1/4 cup extra virgin coconut oil (softened)

Directions:

1. Combine all the ingredients in a bowl. Adjust the salt and sweetener according to taste. Transfer into molds and freeze for an hour before serving.

Double Chocolate Keto Bombs

Servings: 2 dozens

Nutrition facts per 3 pieces: Calories 292 kcal, Fats 31 g, Protein 2.2 g, Net carb 1.3 g

Ingredients:

For the ganache filling

- 1 1/4 teaspoon chocolate extract
- 2 tablespoons, plus 2 teaspoons of heavy cream
- 5 ounces of low-carb chocolate
- 1/2 teaspoon sugar-free vanilla extract

For the chocolate coating

- 2 ounces of unsweetened baking chocolate
- 1 tablespoon sugar substitute
- 3 teaspoons cocoa butter
- 1/8 teaspoon stevia extract
- 1/4 teaspoon of sugar-free vanilla extract

Directions:

1. Put the chocolate in a double boiler and stir until melted.

2. Put the vanilla and cream in a heatproof bowl. Microwave for 2 minutes. Add the melted chocolate and chocolate extract. Mix well and leave for 5 minutes. Cover the bowl with a plastic wrap. Freeze for 12 hours or overnight.

3. Leave the chilled ganache at a room temperature for a couple of minutes. Divide and mold them into balls. Arrange the balls on a plate lined with wax paper. Refrigerate while you are working on the coating.

4. Melt the cocoa butter and chocolate in a double boiler. Add the sweeteners and vanilla. Mix well.

5. Dip each ball into the chocolate coating. Arrange them on a plate lined with wax paper and refrigerate until ready to serve.

Guacamole Healthy Treats

Servings: 6 pieces

Nutrition facts per piece: Calories 156 kcal, Fats 15.2 g, Protein 3.4 g, Net carb 1.4 g

Ingredients:

- 1/2 large avocado
- 2 garlic cloves (crushed)
- 1/2 white onion (diced)
- 1/4 cup butter or ghee (room temperature)
- 4 large bacon slices
- 1 chili pepper (minced)
- Sea salt and freshly ground black to taste
- 1 tablespoon fresh lime juice
- 2 tablespoons freshly chopped cilantro

Directions:

1. Put the bacon slices on a baking tray lined with wax paper. Cook in a preheated oven at 375 degrees for 15 minutes or until golden brown. Trans-

fer to a wire rack and allow to cool. Reserve the drippings and crumble the bacon to be used as breading.

2. Scoop out the meat of the avocado into a bowl. Add the chili pepper, butter, lime juice, cilantro, and crushed garlic. Season with salt and pepper. Mash and mix using a fork until everything is combined. Add the onion and mix thoroughly. Add the bacon drippings from the tray. Mix until combined.

3. Cover the bowl with foil and refrigerate for 30 minutes.

4. Divide the dough into 6 and form them into balls. Roll them in the crumbled bacon and arrange on a tray. Refrigerate for 15 minutes before serving.

Store the leftovers in an airtight container. They will last for a week when refrigerated.

Pecan and Bacon Keto Treats

Servings: 3 pieces

Nutrition facts per 3 pieces: Calories 158 kcal, Fats 17 g, Protein 2 g, Net carb 1 g

Ingredients:

- 1 tablespoon unsalted butter
- 1 slice of bacon
- 2 pecan halves (toasted and chopped)
- A pinch of granulated garlic

Directions:

1. Cut the bacon into 3 slices. Spread butter on each side of the bacon and place it into a pecan. Sprinkle with a little salt and enjoy your treat.

Coco-Choco Candy Cups

Servings: 20 mini cups

Nutrition facts per 2 pieces: Calories 240 kcal, Fats 25 g, Protein 2 g, Net carb 1 g

Ingredients:

- 1/2 cup coconut oil
- 1/2 cup coconut butter
- 3 tablespoons sweetener
- 1/2 cup unsweetened shredded coconut

For the chocolate topping

- 1-ounce unsweetened chocolate
- 1 1/2 ounces cocoa butter
- 1/4 cup cocoa powder
- 1/4 teaspoon vanilla extract
- 1/4 cup powdered sweetener

Directions:

1. Work on the candies first. Arrange 20 mini pa-

per liners in a mini muffin pan. Set aside.

2. Put the coconut oil and coconut butter in a saucepan over low heat. Mix until melted and combined. Add the sweetener and shredded coconut. Mix well. Remove from heat. Divide among the prepared molds. Freeze for an hour.

3. Put the unsweetened chocolate and cocoa butter in a bowl. Put the bowl on top of a pan with simmering water over low heat. Mix until combined and melted. Sift the sweetener into the bowl. Add the cocoa powder. Mix until smooth. Turn off the heat. Add the vanilla extract and mix well.

4. Spoon the melted chocolate mixture on top of the candies. Freeze for 15 minutes before serving.

Put any excess in an airtight container. They will last for a week at a room temperature.

Egg-Free Mini Lemony Tarts

Servings: 24 tarts

Nutrition facts per piece: Calories 101 kcal, Fats 10.3 g, Protein 1.3 g, Net carb 1.08 g

Ingredients:

For the crust

- 3/4 cup dried coconut (finely grated)
- 1 cup almond flour
- 2 tablespoons sugar substitute
- 1 1/2 teaspoons vanilla extract
- 3 tablespoons lemon juice
- A pinch of salt
- 4 1/2 tablespoons butter or ghee (melted)

For the filling

- 1/3 cup fresh lemon juice
- 1/2 cup butter or ghee (room temperature)
- 2 teaspoons lemon extract

- 1/3 cup full-fat coconut milk
- Grated zest of 2 lemons
- 1 teaspoon vanilla extract (sugar-free)
- 1/2 cup sugar substitute
- 1/4 teaspoon salt

Directions:

1. Lightly grease 2 mini muffin pans. Set aside.

2. Put all the ingredients for the crust in a bowl. Mix until combined. Transfer the dough on a wax paper and roll into a log. Slice into 24 parts. Form each part into a ball. Put each ball in the hole of the muffin pan and press at the bottom. Cover with a plastic wrap and chill as you work on the filling.

3. Put the butter in a bowl. Beat using an electric mixer until smooth. Add the sweetener, salt, milk, extracts, lemon juice, and zest. Beat until everything is combined. Taste the mixture and add more sweetener or lemon juice according to preference.

4. Lay the muffin pans on the table. Spoon the filling on top of each crust. Top each with a bit of lemon zest. Put in the fridge for 15 minutes or until ready to serve.

You can serve the excess filling as a pudding. You can also put them into molds, freeze, and turn them into lemon-flavored fat bombs.

Choco Candies with Coconut

Servings: 30 candies

Nutrition facts per piece: Calories 76 kcal, Fats 7.7 g, Protein 0.92 g, Net carb 1 g

Ingredients:

- 1 cup raw cocoa powder
- 1 cup extra virgin coconut oil
- 1/4 cup powdered Erythritol
- A pinch salt
- 1 teaspoon vanilla bean powder
- 1/4 cup coconut and pecan butter (chilled)
- 15 drops stevia extract

Directions:

1. Put the extra virgin coconut oil in a heatproof bowl. Microwave for a minute on a low setting. Stir in the stevia, Erythritol, cocoa powder, and vanilla extract. Take note that it is important to mix the Erythritol with the oil while it is still hot,

otherwise, you'll find it hard to dissolve. Mix thoroughly until there are no lumps.

2. Fill the 1/3 portion of a silicone mold with the chocolate mixture. Once you are done with all the molds, put them in the fridge for 15 minutes.

3. Put half a teaspoon of the coconut and pecan butter on top of the chocolate in each mold. Pour over the rest of the chocolate mixture on top and refrigerate for an hour before serving.

Keep the candies refrigerated. Remove them from the molds when you are ready to eat them. The base is coconut oil, which easily gets soft at a room temperature.

Yummy Keto Rolo

Servings: 12 pieces

Nutrition facts per piece: Calories 118 kcal, Fats 13.2 g, Protein 0.8 g, Net carb 0.8 g

Ingredients:

For the dark chocolate bar

- 1.5 ounces unsweetened baking chocolate (melted)

For the milk chocolate bar

- 1/4-ounce unsweetened baking chocolate (melted)

For the white chocolate bar

- 1 teaspoon toffee extract
- 2 ounces cocoa butter
- Sea salt to taste
- 1/3 cup Swerve confectioners

For the caramel filling

- 6 tablespoons organic butter
- 1/2 cup heavy whipping cream (organic)
- 1 cup Swerve confectioners

Directions:

1. Put the cocoa butter in a heatproof bowl. Microwave for a minute on a high setting. Stir and check every 30 seconds to make sure that it is fully melted. This fat takes a longer time to melt than the traditional kinds. Add the sweetener and mix well. Add the salt and extracts, and stir until combined. Transfer the white chocolate mixture into your molds. Refrigerate for an hour or until set.

2. Gather all the ingredients for the filling before working on it. You have to work fast so that the ingredients won't burn. Heat butter in a saucepan over low heat. Once it boils, immediately add the cream and confectioners. Whisk and scrape the sides to combine everything. Continue whisking until smooth. Turn off the heat.

3. Lay the molds with the chilled white chocolate layer on the table. Scoop the filling into each mold. Top each piece with melted chocolate. Refrigerate until set.

Frozen Cocoa Bombs

Servings: 20 pieces

Nutrition facts per 2 pieces: Calories 48.8 kcal, Fats 5 g, Protein 0.7 g, Net carb 1.1 g

Ingredients:

- 2 tablespoons unsweetened cocoa powder
- 1/4 teaspoon cayenne pepper
- 1 cup coconut milk
- 1 teaspoon cinnamon
- 20 drops stevia extract
- 1 teaspoon unsweetened vanilla extract
- 2 tablespoons powdered Erythritol

Directions:

1. Put the coconut milk in a heatproof bowl. Microwave for several seconds or until slightly warm. This will make it easier for the other ingredients to dissolve. Add the rest of the ingredients. Mix well.

2. Scoop a tablespoon of the mixture into each hole of an ice cube tray. Chill for 2 hours.

Fudgy White Choco Bombs

Servings: 24 pieces

Nutrition facts per piece: Calories 175 kcal, Fats 17.8 g, Protein 2.2 g, Net carb 1.2 g

Ingredients:

- 1/2 cup vanilla protein powder
- 1 15-ounce can coconut milk
- 4 ounces cacao butter
- A pinch salt
- 1/2 cup coconut oil
- 1 teaspoon coconut liquid stevia
- 1 cup coconut butter
- 1 teaspoon vanilla extract
- Unsweetened coconut flakes as toppings

Directions:

1. Put the cacao butter in a sauce pan over low flame. Stir until melted. Add the coconut oil, coconut milk, and coconut butter. Mix well until

combined and free of lumps. Remove from the stove. Stir in the vanilla extract, salt, stevia, and protein powder. Mix until everything is incorporated.

2. Transfer the mixture to a square baking pan lined with parchment paper. Sprinkle coconut flakes on top. Cover and refrigerate overnight.

3. Slice and serve.

You can keep the leftovers at a room temperature.

Spiced Keto Candies

Servings: 6 pieces

Nutrition facts per piece: Calories 372 kcal, Fats 36.98 g, Protein 2.32 g, Net carb 1.7 g

Ingredients:

- 1/2 cup of sweetener
- 8 ounces full-fat cream cheese (room temperature)
- 3/4 cup coconut oil (melted)
- 1 teaspoon ground cinnamon
- 1 teaspoon freshly grated ginger
- 1/2 teaspoon ground nutmeg
- 1/2 teaspoon ground cloves

Directions:

1. Put everything, except the coconut oil, in a food processor. Process until smooth. Gradually add the oil while the machine is running. Continue

mixing until the mixture resembles the consistency of a mayonnaise.

2. Transfer the mixture into 6 small molds with lids. Lock the lids and refrigerate until ready to serve.

Low-Carb Chocolate Bars

Servings: 12 pieces

Nutrition facts per piece: Calories 216 kcal, Fats 22 g, Protein 2 g, Net carb 2 g

Ingredients:

For the coconut layer

- 1/3 cup virgin coconut oil (melted)
- 2 cups shredded coconut (unsweetened)
- 2 drops liquid stevia

For the chocolate layer

- 1 tablespoon coconut oil
- 3 ounces unsweetened baking chocolate
- 2 drops liquid stevia

Directions:

1. Attach the S blade on your food processor. Put all the ingredients for the coco layer. Process until

combined. Scrape the sides and process until the dough is formed.

2. Transfer the dough into a silicone loaf pan. Press it at the bottom. Freeze until set.

3. Put the chocolate and coconut oil in a heatproof bowl. Microwave on a high until melted. Add the sweetener. Mix well.

4. Pour the melted chocolate on top of the chilled coconut layer. Put back in the freezer for half an hour.

5. Remove from the mold and slice into 12 bars. Keep the leftovers in a Ziploc bag and store in the freezer.

Double Chocolate Truffles

Servings: 2 dozens

Nutrition facts per 3 pieces: Calories 292 kcal, Fats 2.8 g, Protein 2.2 g, Net carb 1.3 g

Ingredients:

For the ganache filling

- 2 tablespoons, plus 2 teaspoons heavy cream
- 5 ounces low-carb dark chocolate
- 1 1/4 teaspoon chocolate extract
- 1/2 teaspoon vanilla extract

For the chocolate coating

- ½ ounce cocoa butter
- 2 ounces unsweetened baking chocolate
- 1/4 teaspoon vanilla extract
- 1 tablespoon Swerve confectioners
- 1/8 teaspoon stevia extract

Directions:

1. Prepare the ganache. Melt the chocolate in a double boiler.

2. Put the vanilla and cream in a heatproof bowl. Microwave until the mixture is in the bubbling stage. This means that it is near to boiling point. Add the mixture to the melted chocolate. Stir in the chocolate extract. Leave to temper for 5 minutes. Transfer the hot mixture into a bowl. Put a plastic wrap on top. The plastic must touch the surface of the mixture. Freeze for 6 hours or overnight.

3. Scoop small balls from the chilled ganache. Arrange them on a tray lined with wax paper. Refrigerate while you work on the coating.

4. Melt the chocolate in a double boiler over low heat. Add the cocoa butter. Mix until melted and combined. Remove from heat. Add the vanilla and sweeteners. Mix well.

5. Dip each ball into the melted chocolate mixture. Allow to set and dip one more time for a thicker coating.

You can also opt to roll the ganache in chopped nuts or sprinkle them with a bit of sea salt before dipping into the melted chocolate.

Cheesy Almond Keto Bombs

Servings: 12 pieces

Nutrition facts per piece: Calories 86 kcal, Fats 7 g, Protein 2 g, Net carb 2 g

Ingredients:

- 1 ounce cream cheese
- 4 tablespoons coconut butter
- 1 tablespoon cocoa powder
- 16 grams dark chocolate
- 4 tablespoons almond butter
- 2 tablespoons sugar-free syrup

Directions:

1. Put all the ingredients except for the coconut butter in a heatproof bowl. Microwave until melted while stirring the mixture every 15 seconds to check. Once everything is combined, add the coconut butter, and mix well.

2. Pour the mixture into your molds. Freeze for an hour. Remove from the molds when ready to serve. Keep the leftovers in the fridge because they will easily melt when left at a room temperature.

Chapter 3 – Low-Carb Fat Bomb Recipes with Berries

It is important that you are aware of the right ingredients to use when following a low-carb diet. After trying out the recipes from this book and when you already know the right techniques in creating fat bombs, you can come up with recipes of your own. You can use any ingredient that you want as long as they contain a low amount of carbs.

Vegetables and fruits are quite common in any low-carb diet. Stick with the dark and leafy kinds when choosing veggies because they are low in carbs and high in nutrients. Most green cruciferous veggies that are grown above the ground are suitable for the diet. Anything that grows underground has to be consumed in moderation.

Here's a list of the vegetables that you can eat anytime:

- Leafy greens (contain 0.5 to 5 grams net carbs for every cup) – Kale, beet greens, dandelion, chard, mustard, fennel, endive, chicory, turnip, romaine
- Cruciferous vegetables (contain 3 to 6 grams net carb for every cup) – Cabbage, cauliflower, broccoli, Brussels sprouts
- Fresh herbs (almost no carbs for every 1 to 2 tablespoons)
- Cucumber, chives, celery, leeks, zucchini (contain 2 to 4 grams net carbs for every 1 cup)

The following vegetables have slightly higher carb content at around 3 to 7 grams net carbs for every 1 cup but are still safe to eat on a low-carb diet:

- Green beans
- Asparagus
- Tomatoes
- Bamboo shoots
- Water chestnuts
- Jicama

- Radish
- Mushroom
- Bean sprouts
- Sugar snap peas

Fruits

Berries are among the safest fruits to eat when you are on a low-carb diet. They can help you in sticking to your 30 grams or less carb limit per day. Here's a list of the fruits that you can include in your diet and how much carbs they have for every 100 grams and their average serving sizes.

- Avocado – 1.84 grams (1/2 of the fruit)
- Starfruits – 3.93 grams (1 medium piece)
- Tomato – 2.69 grams (1 piece of small vine type)
- Honeydew melon – 5.68 grams (8 honey-dew balls)
- Cantaloupe – 7.26 grams (7 cantaloupe balls)

- Watermelon – 7.15 grams (8 watermelon balls)
- Rhubarb – 2.74 grams (2 stalks)
- Apricot – 9.12 grams (3 pitted fruits)
- Clementine – 10.32 (1 medium piece)
- Coconut meat – 6.23 grams (1 cup of shredded coconut)
- Lemon – 6.52 grams (2 pieces)
- Kiwi – 11.66 grams (1 1/2 pieces)
- Granny Smith apple – 10.81 grams (3/5 of a medium piece)
- Peach – 8.05 grams (3/4 of a small fruit)
- Plum – 10.02 grams (1 1/2 pieces)

Berries

This chapter features recipes that include berries in the ingredients. Here are some of the berries used in the recipes, including their carb content and health benefits:

1. Blackberries

These berries have been used since the ancient

times in treating gout and other illnesses. They contain high amounts of nutrients, such as manganese, and vitamins C and K. They reduce inflammation, boost the motor, and brain function, and improve the health of your skin. The fruit is also loaded with anthocyanin and ellagic acid that can help in slowing down the growth of cancer by suppressing the mutation of the cell. One cup of raspberries contains 7 grams of net carbs and 8 grams of fiber.

2. Raspberries

They are high in nutrients and low in carbs. Aside from fat bombs, you can also use raspberries in other sweet and savory dishes and treats. They have antioxidant properties that help in fighting inflammation and in protecting your body from harmful free radicals. Raspberries have a high content of polyphenol that helps in preventing the buildup of platelet in the arteries and lowers the blood pressure. A serving of 1/2 cup of the fruit contains 3.5 grams net carbs.

3. Strawberries

The fruit has slightly higher carb content than raspberries and blackberries. You'll get about 5 grams net carbs for every 3/4 cup serving. Always remember to eat them in moderation. Aside from being refreshing, strawberries help in improving your blood sugar and insulin levels.

4. Blueberries

They are rich in vitamin C and antioxidants that are good for the skin. They must also be consumed in moderation because the fruit contains higher amount of carbs than strawberries. They have about 17.4 grams net carbs for every serving of 1 cup. They also have a higher fructose content than the other berries that is why it is important that you limit its intake.

Here are some samples of the fat bomb recipes with different berries as part of the ingredients:

Coconut and Berries Fat Bombs

Servings: 16 small squares

Nutrition facts per 1 square: Calories 170 kcal, Fats 18.7 g, Protein 1.1 g, Net carb 0.8 g

Ingredients:

- 1/2 cup fresh or frozen berries of your choice (raspberries, blackberries, or strawberries)
- 1 cup coconut oil
- 1 tablespoon lemon juice
- 1 cup coconut butter
- 1/2 teaspoon vanilla extract
- 1/2 teaspoon stevia drops

Directions:

1. Heat coconut oil and coconut butter in a pan over medium heat. Stir in the berries if frozen. Mix until combined and the oils are melted.

2. Allow the oil mixture to lightly cool before transferring to a food processor. Add the rest of the ingredients and process until smooth.

3. Pour the mixture into a square pan lined with parchment paper. Put in the fridge for at least an hour. Slice into squares and serve.

Chocolatey Strawberry Swirl Bombs

Servings: 12

Nutrition facts per piece: Calories 99 kcal, Fats 11 g, Protein 0.1 g, Net carb 1 g

Ingredients:

- 2 tablespoons cocoa powder
- 1/4 teaspoon liquid stevia
- 4 tablespoons coconut oil
- 4 tablespoons unsalted butter

For the strawberry swirl

- 1/4 cup strawberries
- 1/4 teaspoon liquid stevia
- 1 tablespoon coconut oil
- 1 tablespoon unsalted butter
- 1 tablespoon heavy cream

Directions:

1. Put the butter in a heatproof bowl. Microwave

until soft. Allow to cool a little before adding the cocoa powder, stevia, and coconut oil. Mix well and set aside.

2. Prepare the strawberry swirl. Put the heavy cream and strawberries in a heatproof bowl. Mash the berries as you mix. Microwave for 10 seconds and set aside.

3. Melt butter in another bowl. Gradually add the warm strawberry mixture, stevia, and coconut oil. Mix using a stick blender until combined.

4. To assemble, pour the chocolate mixture first into your molds. Add the strawberry mixture at the center and swirl using a toothpick. Freeze the fat bombs for 20 minutes before removing from the molds. Put any leftover in an airtight container and store in the freezer.

Blackberries and Cheese Fat Bombs

Servings: 12

Nutrition facts per piece: Calories 392 kcal, Fats 50 g, Protein 4 g, Net carb 1.3 g

Ingredients:

- 1 cup blackberries
- 3 tablespoons mascarpone cheese
- 4 ounces cream cheese (softened)
- Stevia to taste
- 2 ounces macadamia nuts (crushed)
- 1/2 teaspoon lemon juice
- 1/2 teaspoon vanilla extract
- 1 cup coconut butter
- 1 cup coconut oil

Directions:

1. Put the macadamia nuts in the food processor and process until crushed. Transfer to a baking dish and press at the bottom. Bake for 7 minutes

at 325 degrees or until golden brown. Leave until slightly cool.

2. Spread the softened cream cheese on top of the macadamia layer.

3. In a bowl, put the mascarpone cheese, sweetener, vanilla, blackberries, lemon juice, coconut butter, and coconut oil. Mix until smooth. Pour this over the cream cheese layer and spread using a spatula.

4. Cover and freeze for an hour. Slice and serve.

Blueberry and Cheese Fat Bombs

Servings: 16 pieces

Nutrition facts per piece: Calories 231 kcal, Fats 29 g, Protein 3 g, Net carb 2 g

Ingredients:

- 4 ounces Neufchatel cheese (softened)
- 1 cup blueberries
- Liquid stevia to taste
- 1/4 cup coconut cream
- 8 ounces unsalted butter
- 3/4 cup coconut oil

Directions

1. Put the blueberries in a pan and crush them at the bottom.

2. Melt butter in a saucepan over low heat. Stir in the oil. Remove from heat and leave for 5 minutes. Add the rest of the ingredients. Use a hand blender to whisk well. Gradually add stevia

to taste. Pour this on top of the crushed berries. Chill for an hour.

3. Slice and top with whole blueberries before serving.

Note: You can also opt to use pureed berries. To get it done, put the berries, cream cheese, and coconut cream in a blender. Process until pureed. Melt the coconut oil and butter in a saucepan over low heat. Cool for 5 minutes and add stevia to taste. Put the mixture in the blender. Process until everything is combined. Transfer into your molds and freeze for an hour.

Raspberry and Choco Treats

Servings: 14 pieces

Nutrition facts per piece: Calories 164 kcal, Fats 17.1 g, Protein 2.2 g, Net carb 2.6 g

Ingredients:

You have 2 options for the chocolate.

For milder taste, use the quick keto chocolate:

- 100 grams cocoa butter
- 1 teaspoon unsweetened vanilla extract
- 2 tablespoons extra virgin coconut oil
- 300 grams dark chocolate (at least 85 percent)
- Sweetener to taste

Your other option is to make homemade chocolate:

- 4.2 ounces unsweetened dark chocolate (100 percent cacao)

- 1/2 cup cocoa butter
- 1 teaspoon unsweetened vanilla extract
- 3 tablespoons extra virgin coconut oil
- 25 drops stevia extract
- 1/3 cup unsweetened cacao powder
- Powdered Erythritol to taste

For the toppings

- 30 grams almonds (around 25 pieces)
- 1 1/2 cups fresh or frozen raspberries

Directions:

1. Roast the almonds in a pan for 5 minutes. Put each nut into a raspberry. Arrange them on a tray and chill for an hour.

2. If you are using the quick keto chocolate, put all the ingredients in a double boiler. Mix until melted and combined.

3. For the other option, put the coconut oil, cocoa butter, and unsweetened chocolate in a bowl. Put the bowl on top of a pot with boiling water over

low heat. Stir the mixture until melted. Remove from heat. Add the unsweetened cacao, vanilla extract, stevia, and powdered Erythritol. Mix thoroughly.

4. Lay mini muffin paper cups on a tray. Scoop a tablespoon of the chocolate mixture into each cup. Put 2 chilled raspberries in every cup. Scoop another tablespoon of chocolate on top. Refrigerate for 30 minutes or until ready to serve.

These treats will last up to 3 days when stored in the fridge and up to a week when chilled.

Low-Carb Strawberry Cheesecake Delights

Servings: 14 pieces

Nutrition facts per piece: Calories 67 kcal, Fats 7.4 g, Protein 0.96 g, Net carb 0.85 g

Ingredients:

- 1/2 cup strawberries (fresh or frozen)
- 1/4 cup butter or coconut oil (softened)
- 1 tablespoon vanilla extract
- 5.3 ounces cream cheese (room temperature)
- 15 drops liquid stevia

Directions:

1. Cut the butter and cream cheese into small pieces and put them in a bowl. Leave at a room temperature for an hour.

2. Remove the green parts and rinse the strawberries. Put them in a blender and process until

smooth. Add the vanilla extract and stevia. Pulse until combined.

3. Add the strawberry mixture to the bowl of softened cream cheese and butter. Whisk using a hand mixer. You can also use a food processor to make sure that everything is combined.

4. Scoop the mixture into candy or small silicon molds. Freeze for 2 hours. Remove from the molds when ready to serve.

Chapter 4 – Low-Carb Fat Bomb Recipes with Nuts

Nuts are technically fruits but the main difference is that they are not that sweet and soft. They are found inside hard outer shells that you need to crack open to get them. Nuts are generally rich in monounsaturated fatty acids or MUFAs that are good for the heart, except for walnuts.

Nuts and seeds contain a low amount of carbs and are rich in vitamins, minerals, and fiber, which make these 2 ingredients suitable for a low-carb diet. It is easy to over eat these foods since they are easy to consume. You only need to get a handful and pop them into your mouth.

If you want to snack on nuts and seeds, divide them into portions and limit your serving to once or twice a day. They are also used in a variety of low-carb recipes, including fat bombs.

Here are some of the healthiest nuts that you can include in your diet, including the amount of carbohydrates that they contain for every 28 grams serving:

1. Macadamia nuts (1.5 g net carbs, 2.4 g fiber, 3.9 g total carbs)

These nuts have the highest amount of fat among the other kinds of nuts. Around 78 percent of the fats in these nuts are MUFA, which is among the highest as compared to other nuts. They are effective in increasing the levels of your good cholesterol and in decreasing the levels of the bad cholesterol.

2. Almonds (2.6 g net carbs, 3.5 g fiber, 6.1 g total carbs)

You can get 37 percent of the Recommended Dietary Allowance for vitamin E from almonds. It helps in decreasing the levels of your bad cholesterol. It also works by improving the condition of your heart. They contain the highest amount of protein among all nuts and seeds. You'll get 6 grams of protein for every serving of almonds.

3. Pecans (1.2 g net carbs, 2.7 g fiber, 3.9 g total carbs)

They contain the lowest amount of carbs among all nuts. They are also a good source of zinc. Pecans help in lowering your blood pressure and they also have antioxidant properties.

4. Walnuts (2 g net carbs, 1.9 g fiber, 3.9 g total carbs)

They are rich in omega-3 fatty acids. Walnuts lower your LDL particles and reduce your LDL cholesterol. It also helps in improving the function of your artery.

5. Brazil nuts (1.4 g net carbs, 2.1 g fiber, 3.5 g total carbs)

These nuts contain a high amount of selenium that helps in keeping your thyroid function healthy. It is important that you don't get too much selenium in your system so make sure that you limit your intake of Brazil nuts. When taken in moderation, the nuts can help in protecting your cells from free radicals and decrease your risk of inflammation.

6. Pistachios (5 g net carbs, 2.9 g fiber, 7.9 g total carbs)

You will get 24 percent of your daily vitamin B6 requirement from a serving of these nuts. They help in improving the values of your lipid and blood sugar. Pistachios are also beneficial to people with diabetes because they can lower the levels of your blood sugar, triglyceride, and cholesterol.

7. Hazelnuts (2 g net carbs, 2.7 g fiber, 4.7 g total carbs)

They help in improving your lipid profile by giving sufficient amount of vitamin E. They boost the levels of your good cholesterol and decrease the levels of the bad type.

Here are the recipes that you can try with nuts as one of the main ingredients. You can try using other nuts to tweak each recipe, but make sure that you adjust the nutritional information accordingly.

Chewy Bombs with Macadamia

Servings: 6 pieces

Nutrition facts per piece: Calories 267 kcal, Fats 28 g, Protein 3 g, Net carb 3 g

Ingredients:

- 2 tablespoons unsweetened cocoa powder
- 1/4 cup heavy cream (if you want a dairy-free recipe, use coconut oil)
- 2 tablespoons sugar substitute
- 2 ounces cocoa butter
- 4 ounces macadamia nuts (chopped)

Directions:

1. Put the cocoa butter in a saucepan over low heat. Stir until melted. Add the cocoa butter. Mix well. Stir in the sugar substitute. Mix until everything in melted and combined. Stir in the chopped nuts.

2. Remove from heat. Add the cream and mix well. Leave to cool.

3. Pour the mixture into molds. Refrigerate until set or until ready to serve.

Walnut Keto Delights

Servings: 36 squares

Nutrition facts per piece: Calories 170 kcal, Fats 17.4 g, Protein 2.2 g, Net carb 1 g

Ingredients:

- 1 cup all-natural roasted almond butter
- 1/2 cup ghee (melted)
- 1/2 cup full-fat coconut milk (frozen overnight)
- 1 cup creamy coconut butter
- 1 tablespoon pure almond extract
- 1 cup coconut oil
- 2 teaspoons chai spice
- 1/4 cup ghee
- 1/4 teaspoons sea salt
- 1/4 cup walnuts (chopped)

Directions:

1. Line a greased square baking pan with parchment paper. Set aside.

2. Put the ghee in a saucepan over low flame. Stir until melted. Set aside.

3. In a bowl, put all the ingredients, except for the walnuts and melted ghee. Mix using an electric mixer on a low speed setting. Gradually add the speed to a high until the mixture becomes fluffy and light. Set the mixer's speed back on a low. Add the melted ghee and mix until everything is combined.

4. Pour the mixture and spread evenly in the prepared pan. Sprinkle with the chopped nuts. Put in the refrigerator overnight.

5. Slice into 36 squares. Serve and enjoy.

Orange and Nuts Low-Carb Delights

Servings: 25 pieces

Nutrition facts per piece: Calories 86.4 kcal, Fats 8.4 g, Protein 1.5 g, Net carb 1.5 g

Ingredients:

- 125 grams of dark chocolate (85 percent cocoa)
- 1 tablespoon of orange peel and fresh orange extract
- 1 teaspoon cinnamon
- 15 drops of liquid stevia
- 150 grams walnuts (chopped)
- 1/4 cup of extra virgin coconut oil

Directions:

1. Put the chocolate in a heatproof bowl. Microwave until melted. Gradually add the coconut oil and cinnamon. Add the remaining ingredients.

Mix until well combined. Transfer into molds and refrigerate for an hour or until set.

Choco-Macadamia Treats

Servings: 6 pieces

Nutrition facts per piece: Calories 267 kcal, Fats 28 g, Protein 6 g, Net carb 3 g

Ingredients:

- 2 tablespoons unsweetened cocoa powder
- 1/4 cup heavy cream
- 4 ounces of chopped macadamia nuts
- 2 ounces of cocoa butter
- 2 tablespoons of sugar substitute

Directions:

1. Put the cocoa butter in a saucepan over low heat. Stir until melted. Remove from heat. Add the cocoa powder. Mix until combined. Add the remaining ingredients and mix well. Transfer to molds and refrigerate for at least 30 minutes before serving.

Pumpkin Treats with Pecans

Servings: 8 pieces

Nutrition facts per piece: Calories 227 kcal, Fats 39 g, Protein 11 g, Net carb 1 g

Ingredients:

- 1/2 cup pumpkin (pureed)
- 1/4 cup chopped pecans
- 1/2 cup unsalted butter
- 1/8 teaspoon sea salt
- 12 drops liquid stevia
- 1 teaspoon cinnamon
- 8 ounces Neufchatel cheese
- 1/2 teaspoons pumpkin spice
- 2 teaspoons vanilla extract

Directions:

1. Melt butter in a saucepan over low heat while whisking often. Add the pureed pumpkin as you continue to whisk. Stir in the pecans, stevia,

cream cheese, and spices. Whisk until smooth. Add the vanilla extract and mix well. Turn off the heat.

2. Transfer the mixture to a baking pan lined with wax paper. You can opt to add more pecans on top. Freeze overnight. Pull the wax paper before slicing.

Nutty Choco Treats

Servings: 12 pieces

Nutrition facts per piece: Calories 124 kcal, Fats 12 g, Protein 4 g, Net carb 1.6 g

Ingredients:

- 1/2 cup peanut butter
- 4 tablespoons coconut oil
- 4 tablespoons cocoa powder
- 1/4 tablespoon cinnamon
- Stevia to taste
- Sea salt to taste
- 1 teaspoon vanilla extract
- 1/4 cup walnuts (chopped)

Directions:

1. Put the coconut oil in a heatproof bowl and microwave for 50 seconds or until melted. Set aside.

2. In another bowl, put the vanilla, cocoa, and stevia. Mix well. Fold in the nuts. Transfer to a pan and spread using a spatula.

3. Combine the peanut butter and cinnamon. Pour this on top of the chocolate layer. Sprinkle sea salt on top. Freeze for 20 minutes.

4. Slice and serve.

Note: You can tweak the recipe by using other nuts, such as almonds, macadamia, and pecans.

Macadamia Coconut Bombs

Servings: 12 pieces

Nutrition facts per piece: Calories 188 kcal, Fats 20g, Protein 2 g, Net carb 1.2 g

Ingredients:

For the crust

- 4 tablespoons almond butter
- 4 ounces macadamia nuts
- A dash of salt

For the coconut layer

- 6 tablespoons coconut oil (melted)
- 1/4 cup shredded coconut

For the chocolate layer

- 2 tablespoons coconut oil
- 4 tablespoons cocoa powder
- Liquid stevia to taste

Directions:

1. Prepare the crust. Put the macadamia nuts and salt in a food processor and process until finely ground. Transfer to a bowl. Add the almond butter and mix until combined. Press the mixture at the bottom of a pan.

2. Combine the coconut oil and shredded coconut in a bowl. Pour over the crust, press, and set aside.

3. In a bowl, mix the coconut oil and cocoa powder until smooth. Add stevia according to preference. Pour this over the top layer and use a spatula to flatten and spread it out. Freeze for a couple of hours.

Pecan Treats with Stuffing

Servings: 1

Nutrition facts: Calories 150 kcal, Fats 31 g, Protein 11 g, Net carb 0.8 g

Ingredients:

- 1 ounce cream cheese
- 1/2 teaspoon unsalted butter
- 4 pecan halves
- A pinch of sea salt
- Flavor of choice

Directions:

1. Preheat the oven to 350 degrees. Toast the pecans for 10 minutes. Leave to cool.

2. Soften the cream cheese and butter in a bowl. Add your preferred flavored. It can be anything from vegetables, herbs, or spices. Mix until combined and creamy. Spread the filling in between the pecan halves.

3. Sprinkle with sea salt before serving.

Choco Walnut Delight Bombs

Servings: 8

Nutrition facts per piece: Calories 247 kcal, Fats 29 g, Protein 3 g, Net carb 1 g

Ingredients:

- 1/2 cup almond butter
- 4 tablespoons unsalted butter
- 1/2 cup coconut oil
- 2 tablespoons walnuts (chopped)
- Sea salt to taste
- 6 drops liquid stevia
- Dark chocolate for topping

Directions:

1. Put all the ingredients in a heatproof bowl. Microwave for 30 seconds. Mix well until combined. Pour into molds and freeze for at least 1 hour.

2. Drizzle with melted chocolate on top. You can also opt to sprinkle the fat bombs with coarsely chopped walnuts.

Spiced Pistachio Fast Bombs

Servings: 36 pieces

Nutrition facts per piece: Calories 170 kcal, Fats g, Protein g, Net carb 1.5 g

Ingredients:

- 1/4 cup pistachios (remove shells and chop)
- 1/2 cup chopped cacao butter (melted)
- 1 cup coconut butter
- 1 cup almond butter
- 1 cup coconut oil (firm)
- 1/4 teaspoon sea salt
- 2 teaspoons Chai spice
- 1/4 cup ghee
- 1/4 teaspoon almond extract
- 1 tablespoon vanilla extract
- 1/2 cup frozen coconut milk

Directions:

1. Melt the cacao butter in a saucepan over low heat while stirring often.

2. In a bowl, put the coconut oil, coconut butter, almond butter, coconut milk, ghee, extracts, salt, and Chai spice. Mix using an electric mixer set on low speed. Gradually increase the speed until everything is combined and the mixture is fluffy. Set the speed back to low. Add the melted cacao butter and mix for 3 minutes.

3. Spread the mixture in a pan lined with wax paper. Sprinkle the chopped pistachios on top. Cover the pan and put in the fridge for 5 hours or overnight.

Chapter 5 - Ketogenic Specific Fat Bomb Recipes

The state of ketosis happens when your body no longer gets sufficient supply of carbohydrates. Your body turns to ketosis to process the energy you need. Your body doesn't produce ketones when you are on a regular diet because you don't need them. Instead, your system decides how much fat it will burn.

When you are in the state of ketosis, your body automatically burns fat due to the lack of carbs and produces ketones. The end result will give your body the fuel that it needs. This is safe for as long as there is no ketones build-up, which will create an imbalance in the chemical components of your blood. Ketones build-up often leads to dehydration.

It is important that you educate yourself about the diet before committing to it. You have to know what to eat, what portions, and how often. You must also know the ingredients to avoid when following a low-carb diet.

The state of ketosis is the main cause why you lose weight when you are on this kind of diet. It helps in maintaining your muscles as you shed off the fat. It also suppresses your appetite. As long as you are healthy and you are not suffering from diabetes, you will likely enter this state after 3 days of taking less than 50 grams of carbs each day. Ketosis is one benefit of a low-carb diet, such as ketogenic diet, but you can also achieve this state through fasting.

Having too much ketones in the system is not healthy. To avoid this, you need to regularly monitor the level of your ketones. You can buy test strips to check your blood or urine at the comfort of your home. If you have diabetes, ask the help of an instructor on how to use blood sugar meters that are specifically made for this condition. To be safe, you can always ask the help of your doctor to explain your options and how to monitor the ketone levels in your blood.

What is the effect of a ketone build-up? When the ketones build up in your blood, you will be at a risk of developing ketoacids. The condition is dangerous and can lead to a coma, or in some cases, death. If you aren't diabetic, you are prone to get ketoacid from alcoholism, starvation, and an overactive thyroid. People with diabetes can get DKA or diabetic ketoacid when they get sick or injured, dehydration, and lack or insufficient doses of insulin.

These are the symptoms of ketoacids:

- Peeing often
- Getting tired fast
- Feeling confused
- Having a fruity-smelling breath
- Having trouble breathing
- Dry mouth/feeling thirsty
- Aches in the stomach and belly

- Throwing up
- Flushed or dry skin

DKA may start slow but it becomes dangerous when you begin throwing up. It speeds up the process and might lead to risky complications if not treated properly and on time. If you experience throwing up at this point and you are diabetic, do not wait for more than an hour before you seek your doctor's help.

In order to prevent having ketoacids, stick to your goal of experiencing nutritional ketosis. This is the state wherein your body burns fat instead of glucose to supply your system with energy. This is achieved by removing most sugar and starches from your diet. You will replace them with healthy fats and carbs.

Ketosis is a normal chemical reaction. You experience this everyday even when on a regular diet, but it happens briefly so you remain unaware of it. A low-carb diet prolongs the duration when your body enters this state and allows you to experience its health benefits.

How would you know that you are already in the state of nutritional ketosis? This is the why you need to measure your blood glucose and ketones. Your blood ketones must stay within the range of 0.5 to 3.0 millimoles per liter in order to stay in the state of nutritional ketosis.

To easily get into the state of nutritional ketosis, you have to know your daily macronutrient requirement. This will depend on the following factors:

- The ketogenic ratio suited for your age, weight, and level of physical activities
- Your calorie requirement
- Your protein requirement
- Your fluid intake

There are online macro calculators that you can use to know and monitor this requirement. After accessing the calculator, you will be asked to fill in your age, gender, and whether or not you are physically active.

Getting Keto-Adapted

The beginning is the hardest part of any low-carb diet. Through the days, you will get used to the process and you will eventually get keto-adapted. Keto-adaptation occurs as your system processes the fat-based sources and turns them into fuel. When you reach this point, your body produces more ketones from the partially broken-down fats. These ketones will enter your bloodstream. They will be distributed to the parts of your body where glucose used to flow, most of which will go into your brain.

You have to help your body perform normal functions despite the little amount of glucose that it is getting. Before you get keto-adapted, note that you will be prone to experiencing keto flu symptoms, which signal that your body is still trying to adjust. You might feel unwell but you can make up for it by eating lots of healthy fats, staying hydrated, and taking supplements.

When you are already keto-adapted, you will no longer get the keto flu symptoms. You will have more energy to perform your daily activities and your body will have an improved mood and condition. It happens as your glycogen storage in the muscles and in your liver decreases, and your body has lesser amount of excess water.

If you are intent on losing weight, your goal is to attain optimal ketosis. Make sure that you know your daily macro requirement. Follow the limits no matter how hard it seems. This is the point where fat bombs can help you. They are mostly made of fat that can easily fill your cravings and make you feel full at a faster rate.

The following fat bomb recipes will help you maintain the state of optimal ketosis longer:

Basic Fat Bomb Recipe

Servings: 24 pieces

Nutrition facts per piece: Calories 95 kcal, Fats 10.1 g, Protein 1.1 g, Net carb 0.2 g

Ingredients:

For the coating

- 1 teaspoon lemon extract
- 1/2 cup cocoa butter (melted)
- 1/4 teaspoon sea salt
- 2/3 cup of Swerve confectioners

For the filling

- 8 tablespoons coconut oil
- 1/2 cup of lemon juice
- 1 tablespoon lemon peel (finely grated)
- 4 eggs
- 1 cup of sweetener

Directions:

1. In a bowl, put all the ingredients for the coating and mix until combined. Transfer to your molds. Refrigerate for an hour.

2. Put all the ingredients for the filling in a saucepan over medium heat. Whisk until heated but do not bring to a boil. Strain to a bowl. Put this bowl on top of any container that contains ice. Occasionally whisk the filling until completely cool.

3. Add filling to each truffle. Refrigerate for at least 30 minutes before serving.

Walnut Keto Treats

Servings: 4 pieces

Nutrition facts per piece: Calories 176.32 kcal, Fats 17.77 g, Protein 1.26 g, Net carb 0.5 g

Ingredients:

- 1 tablespoon of walnut halves (chopped and toasted)
- 1 tablespoon unsweetened cocoa powder
- A dash of sea salt
- 1 tablespoon heavy whipping cream
- 2 tablespoons coconut oil (melted)
- 1 tablespoon of sweetener

Directions:

1. Put all the ingredients in a bowl. Mix well until combined and creamy. Transfer to a pan lined with wax paper. Refrigerate for 2 hours. Break into pieces and serve.

Note: You can tweak the recipe to come up with other flavors by using other nuts, such as chestnuts, macadamia, pecans, hazelnuts, and almonds.

Lemon-Flavored Cheesecake Bombs

Servings: 8 pieces

Nutrition facts per piece: Calories 106 kcal, Fats 11 g, Protein 1 g, Net carb 0.25 g

Ingredients:

- 4 ounces cream cheese (softened)
- 4 tablespoons unsalted butter (softened)
- 1 tablespoon lemon zest (finely grated)
- 1/4 cup coconut oil (melted)
- Stevia to taste
- 1 teaspoon lemon juice
- Lemon extract (optional)

Directions:

1. Put all the ingredients in a bowl. Mix until smooth. Transfer to your molds. Freeze for 2 hours or overnight.

2. Sprinkle the fat bombs with lemon zest before serving.

Breakfast Truffles

Servings: 6 pieces

Nutrition facts per piece: Calories 185 kcal, Fats 18.4 g, Protein 5 g, Net carb 0.2 g

Ingredients:

- 1/4 cup butter (softened)
- 2 eggs (hard boiled)
- 4 bacon slices
- 1/4 teaspoon of sea salt
- Freshly ground black pepper to taste
- 2 tablespoons of mayonnaise

Directions:

1. Arrange the bacon slices on a tray. Bake them in a preheated oven at 375 degrees for 15 minutes. Set aside to cool.

2. Peel the hard-boiled eggs and mash them using a fork. Add the mayonnaise. Mix well. Season with

salt and pepper. Add the bacon grease. Mix until combined. Refrigerate for 30 minutes.

3. Break the bacon into small pieces once cooled.

4. Form balls from the batter. Roll each in the crumbled bacon. Arrange the balls on a tray and refrigerate until ready to serve.

Leftovers can last for a week when stored in an airtight container and placed in the fridge.

Energy-Boosting Bulletproof Bombs

Servings: 20 pieces

Nutrition facts per piece: Calories 77 kcal, Fats 8.1 g, Protein 0.8 g, Net carb 0.5 g

Ingredients:

- 1/4 cup butter (or extra virgin coconut oil)
- 1 cup creamed coconut milk (softened)
- 2 tablespoons raw and unsweetened cocoa powder
- 15 drops liquid stevia extract
- 2 tablespoons MCT oil
- 1/2 cup strong brewed coffee
- 1/4 cup powdered Erythritol
- 1 teaspoon rum extract (optional)

Directions:

1. Put the cocoa powder, butter, MCT oil, softened coconut milk, stevia, and powdered Erythritol in a blender. Process until smooth. Make sure that the

brewed coffee is lukewarm and not hot before pouring it into the blender. Process until smooth.

2. Transfer the mixture to an ice cream maker. Process for 30 to 60 minutes depending on the manufacturer's instructions. This will make the mixture creamy and smooth.

3. Scoop less than 2 tablespoons of the mixture into each mold. You can proceed with this step and scoop the mixture directly into the molds after you are done with the first step if you don't have an ice cream maker.

4. Put in the freezer for 3 hours. Serve and enjoy.

Coco Butter Bombs with Nutmeg

Servings: 10 balls

Nutrition facts per piece: Calories 341 kcal, Fats 3.19 g, Protein 0.33 g, Net carb 0.53 g

Ingredients:

- 1 cup full-fat coconut milk
- 1 cup coconut butter
- 1 teaspoon stevia powder extract (adjust according to taste)
- 1 cup coconut shreds
- 1/2 teaspoon cinnamon
- 1/2 teaspoon nutmeg
- 1 teaspoon vanilla extract

Directions:

1. Put all the ingredients, except for the shredded coconut, in a double boiler over medium flame. Mix well until everything is combined and melted. Remove from heat. Allow to cool a little before

putting the bowl inside the refrigerator for an hour.

2. Form 1-inch sized balls from the dough. Roll them in the coconut shreds until all sides are completely covered. Arrange on a plate and put in the fridge for an hour or until ready to serve.

Nutty Vanilla Truffles

Servings: 14 pieces

Nutrition facts per piece: Calories 132 kcal, Fats 14.4 g, Protein 0.79 g, Net carb 0.6 g

Ingredients:

- 1 cup unsalted macadamia nuts
- 15 drops of stevia extract (adjust according to taste)
- 1/4 cup of extra virgin coconut oil (melted)
- 2 tablespoons of powdered sweetener
- 2 teaspoons of sugar-free vanilla extract
- 1/4 cup of softened butter

Directions:

1. Put the macadamia nuts in a blender. Pulse until smooth. Transfer to a bowl. Add the butter, coconut oil, extracts, and sweeteners. Mix well.

2. Transfer the mixture into molds. Refrigerate for an hour.

3. Remove the fat bombs from the molds and serve.

Note: You can use other nuts, such as hazelnuts, pecan, chestnuts, almonds, and walnut. You can also tweak its flavor by using other extracts, such as fruits, herbs, ginger, and lemon.

Spicy Keto Bombs

Servings: 10

Nutrition facts per piece: Calories 120 kcal, Fats 12.8 g, Protein 0.5 g, Net carb 0. 70 g

Ingredients:

- 75 grams of coconut butter (softened)
- 75 grams of coconut oil (softened)
- 1 teaspoon sweetener
- 1/2 teaspoon dried powdered ginger
- 25 grams of unsweetened shredded coconut

Directions:

1. Put all the ingredients in a bowl. Mix until the sweetener is dissolved and everything is combined. Pour into molds. Refrigerate for 10 minutes before serving.

Vanilla-Macadamia Healthy Bombs

Servings: 14 pieces

Nutrition facts per piece: Calories 132 kcal, Fats 14.4 g, Protein 0.79 g, Net carb 0.6 g

Ingredients:

- 1 cup unsalted macadamia nuts
- 2 teaspoons sugar-free vanilla extract
- 15 drops of vanilla stevia extract
- 2 tablespoons of sweetener
- 1/4 cup of extra virgin coconut oil
- 1/4 cup butter

Directions:

1. Put the macadamia nuts in a food processor. Pulse until smooth.

2. Put the coconut oil and butter in a heatproof bowl. Microwave until melted. Stir until combined. Add the vanilla extract and sweetener. Mix

well. Transfer into molds. Put in the fridge for 30 minutes or until set before serving.

Cheesy Raspberry Keto Bombs

Servings: 48 pieces

Nutrition facts per 3 pieces: Calories 81 kcal, Fats 8.6 g, Protein 1 g, Net carb 0.6 g

Ingredients:

- 3 teaspoons raspberry extract
- 8 ounces cream cheese (room temperature)
- 1 teaspoon of vanilla stevia
- 1/2 cup powdered Erythritol
- A pinch of salt
- 1/4 cup coconut oil (melted)
- 2 tablespoons heavy cream
- 1 1/2 cup chocolate chips (sugar-free)
- A few drops of natural red food coloring

Directions:

1. Put the cream cheese and powdered Erythritol in a bowl. Mix using an electric mixer on a low speed setting until smooth. Add the raspberry ex-

tract, heavy cream, salt, and vanilla stevia. Mix in the food coloring. Mix until blended. Gradually add the coconut oil. Scrape the sides of the bowl and continue mixing until everything is incorporated.

2. Cover the bowl and put in the fridge for an hour. Scoop about 48 balls and arrange them on a tray lined with parchment paper. Chill for an hour.

3. Melt the chocolate chips. Dip each ball into the melted chocolate and arrange them on the tray. Put in the fridge for an hour or until ready to serve.

Healthy Macha Bombs

Servings: 32 pieces

Nutrition facts per piece: Calories 132 kcal, Fats 14.4 g, Protein 0.79 g, Net carb 0.6 g

Ingredients:

For the truffles

- 1 cup coconut butter (creamy)
- 1 cup coconut oil (firm)
- 1/4 teaspoon ground cinnamon
- 1/2 cup full-fat coconut milk (refrigerated overnight)
- 1 teaspoon pure vanilla extract
- 1/4 teaspoon Himalayan salt
- 1/2 teaspoon macha green tea powder

For the coating

- 1 tablespoon macha green tea powder

- 1 cup unsweetened coconut (finely shredded)

Directions:

1. Put all the ingredients for the truffles in a bowl. Make sure that both the coconut cream and coconut oil is firm before adding them in. If not, refrigerate them for a few more minutes before proceeding with the step. Mix using an electric mixer on a high speed until it is airy and light. Refrigerate for an hour.

2. Combine the macha powder and shredded coconut in a bowl. Set aside.

3. Scoop 32 small balls from the firm truffles. Roll each ball in your palms and roll in the coconut and macha mixture until all sides are coated.

4. Serve and enjoy.

Put the leftovers in an airtight container. They will last up to 2 weeks when refrigerated. Leave at a room temperature for 15 minutes before eating them.

Chewy Keto Treats

Servings: 12 pieces

Nutrition facts per piece: Calories 172 kcal, Fats 19.6 g, Protein 0.4 g, Net carb 0.7 g

Ingredients:

- 1/4 cup organic cocoa powder
- 1/4 cup full-fat coconut milk
- 1/4 cup Swerve confectioners
- 1 cup coconut oil (softened)
- 1/2 teaspoon sea salt
- 1 teaspoon vanilla extract
- 1/2 teaspoon almond extract

Directions:

1. Put the coconut milk and coconut oil in a bowl. Use a stand mixer set on a high speed to combine the 2. Continue mixing for about 6 minutes. Turn the setting to low speed. Add the rest of the ingredients. Mix until everything is combined. Turn the

speed of the mixer to high and mix for a couple of minutes. Add more sweetener if desired.

2. Transfer the mixture into a loaf pan lined with parchment paper. Chill for 15 minutes.

3. Remove from the pan. Peel the parchment paper and slice into squares.

4. Store in an airtight container. Refrigerate until ready to serve. The fudge will easily liquefy when left in a warm place.

Conclusion

Thank you again for purchasing this book!

I hope this book was able to help you understand what you need to know to gain the most benefits from a low-carb diet. I hope that this book gives you ideas about the ingredients that you can try to include when you make your own fat bomb recipes.

For now, head on to the grocery and start making the fat bomb recipes featured in this book. They are easy to prepare and most of the ingredients are easy to find. These versatile treats make the perfect snacks and instant energy booster whenever you need it. You can make them ahead of time and store them properly so that they can last for 1 to 2 weeks.

Once again, don't forget to grab a copy of your FREE BONUS book "Super Foods For Super Health". If you are interested in learning more about the easily accessible super foods that you could incorporate into your diet and transform your overall health, then this book is for you.

Just go to http://bit.ly/superfoods-gift

Thank you and good luck!

Thank you!

Before you go, I just wanted to say thank you for purchasing my book.

You could have picked from dozens of other books on the same topic but you took a chance and chose this one.

So, a HUGE thanks to you for getting this book and for reading all the way to the end.

Now I wanted to ask you for a small favor. **Could you please take just a few minutes to leave a review for this book on Amazon?**

This feedback will help me continue to write the type of books that will help you get the results you want. So if you enjoyed it, please let me know! (-:

www.ingramcontent.com/pod-product-compliance
Lightning Source LLC
Chambersburg PA
CBHW052056110526
44591CB00013B/2241